Off

Hammerheads

and Other Sharks

Concept and Product Development: Editorial Options, Inc.
Series Designer: Karen Donica
Book Author: Steven Otfinoski

**For information on other World Book
products, visit us at our Web site at
http://www.worldbook.com**

**For information on sales to schools and libraries
in the United States, call 1-800-975-3250.**

**For information on sales to schools and libraries
in Canada, call 1-800-837-5365.**

World Book, Inc.
233 N. Michigan Ave.
Chicago, IL 60601

Library of Congress Cataloging-in-Publication Data

Otfinoski, Steven.
    Hammerheads and other sharks / [book author, Steven Otfinoski].
       p. cm.—(World Book's animals of the world)
    Summary: Questions and answers explore the world of sharks, with an emphasis on
    hammerhead sharks.
    ISBN 0-7166-1210-0 -- ISBN 0-7166-1200-3 (set)
    1. Hammerhead sharks—Juvenile literature. 2. Sharks—Juvenile literature. [1. Hammerhead
    sharks—Miscellanea. 2. Sharks—Miscellanea. 3. Questions and answers.] I. World Book, Inc.
    II. Title. III. Series.

    QL638.95.S7 083 2000
    597.3—dc21

Printed in Singapore

1 2 3 4 5 6 7 8 9 05 04 03 02 01 00

World Book's Animals of the World

Hammerheads
and Other Sharks

Why do people think I'm a hardhead?

World Book, Inc.
A Scott Fetzer Company
Chicago

Contents

Which shark looks like a lumberjack's helper?

Why am I a whale of a shark?

What Is a Shark?

A shark is a very special kind of fish. This hammerhead is just 1 of about 370 known species of sharks. Others are makos, great whites, sand tigers, and dogfish.

What makes sharks so special? For one thing, they do not have bony skeletons like the fish you are probably familiar with. Instead, sharks have skeletons made of cartilage *(KAHR tuh lihj)*. Cartilage is light and flexible, like a plastic drinking straw.

Most sharks have bodies shaped like torpedoes. Their smooth shape and powerful fins make them excellent swimmers. A shark has stiff side fins. These fins act like underwater wings as a shark's tail pushes its body forward. Large fins on a shark's back keep it from rolling over.

All sharks are carnivores *(KAHR nuh vawrz),* or meat-eaters. Most have razor-sharp teeth made for tearing the flesh of prey. Sharks mainly eat other fish. Some even eat other sharks!

Hammerhead shark

Where in the World's Oceans Do Sharks Live?

You can find sharks in all the oceans of the world. The big difference in where sharks live is how close to the shore they get and how deep into the ocean they swim.

Some sharks live in deep ocean waters far from land. Other sharks swim into shallow, coastal waters to hunt for prey. Swimmers need to watch out for sharks that come close to shore!

A number of sharks live and hunt for food on the ocean floor. Others stay near the surface of the water, finding food there.

Look at the diagram. It shows the different depths at which sharks live and how far from shore they swim. Which sharks might you see from a boat close to shore? Which ones might you never see—unless you had special underwater diving equipment?

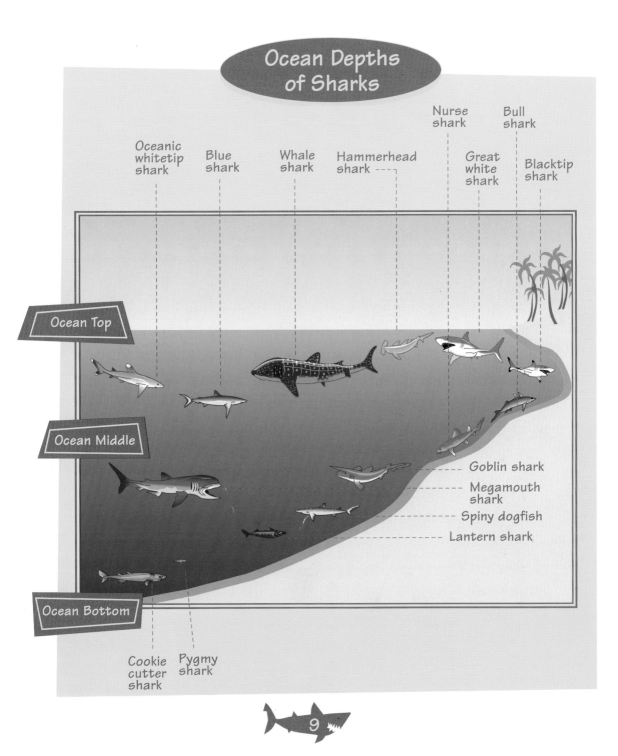

Ocean Depths of Sharks

Oceanic whitetip shark

Blue shark

Whale shark

Hammerhead shark

Nurse shark

Bull shark

Great white shark

Blacktip shark

Ocean Top

Ocean Middle

Goblin shark

Megamouth shark

Spiny dogfish

Lantern shark

Ocean Bottom

Cookie cutter shark

Pygmy shark

9

Do Hammerheads Really Look Like Hammers?

They certainly do! A hammerhead has a flattened head with two ends that stick out like the head of a hammer. On each end is an eye and a nostril.

Hammerheads may look strange, but their oddly shaped heads are actually very useful. Their widely spaced eyes give hammerheads a very broad range of vision. This helps them see their prey. Also, widely spaced nostrils help these sharks figure out where the scent of prey is coming from. Their flat heads allow hammerheads to swim faster and better.

There are nine different species of hammerhead sharks. Different species have heads with slightly different shapes and bodies of different sizes. The bonnethead is the smallest at 5 feet (1.5 meters) in length. The great hammerhead is the largest. It can grow to a length of about 20 feet (6.1 meters).

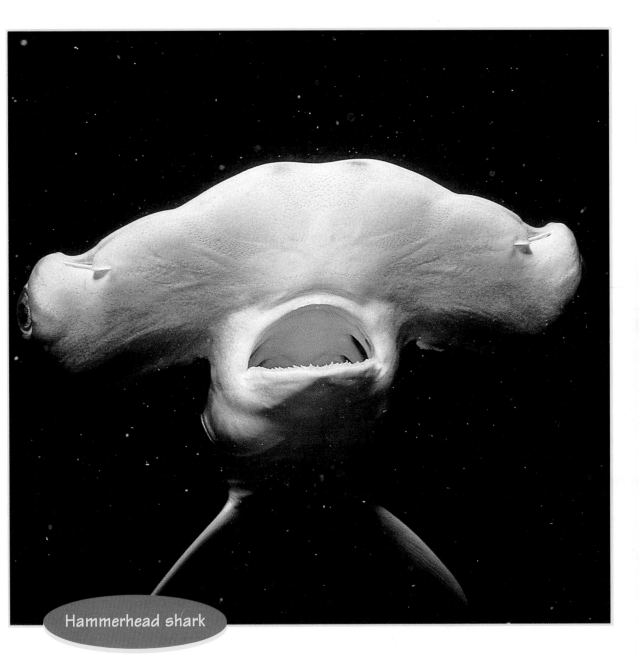

Hammerhead shark

Do Hammerheads Lay Eggs?

Hammerheads do not lay eggs as most fish and some other sharks do. Instead they give birth to live young. This is somewhat like the way mammals—such as cats and dogs—have babies.

Each fertilized egg develops inside a separate sac. The sac is inside the mother and attached to her by a cord. Inside the egg is a material called yolk. Yolk provides nutrients that sharks need to grow. The young hatch inside the mother and keep growing. When they are ready for birth, the young leave the mother's body.

Hammerheads give birth to about 40 young at a time. The young are called pups. And they are tiny versions of adult hammerheads. Shark pups are born ready to swim and feed themselves. They are not, however, ready to protect themselves. And shark pups get no protection from their parents. Alone, many shark pups fall prey to larger sharks and other dangers of the deep.

Young hammerhead

13

Why Are Hammerheads Always on the Move?

If the hammerhead shark were not constantly moving, it would not be able to breathe. It would also have trouble staying afloat in the water.

Hammerheads do not have lungs. But they still need oxygen to breathe, just as you do. They get the oxygen from the water. Hammerheads breathe by taking water in through their mouths and forcing it out through their gills. Swimming keeps the water—and the oxygen—flowing through the hammerhead. Many kinds of sharks beside hammerheads need to keep moving to breathe.

Most fish have swim bladders. These are internal body sacs that fill with air. The air-filled sac helps keep the fish afloat in the water. Hammerheads and other sharks do not have these sacs. Instead, they have large livers filled with oil. Oil is lighter than water, so this helps when it comes to staying afloat. But it is not enough. The motion of swimming prevents sharks from sinking.

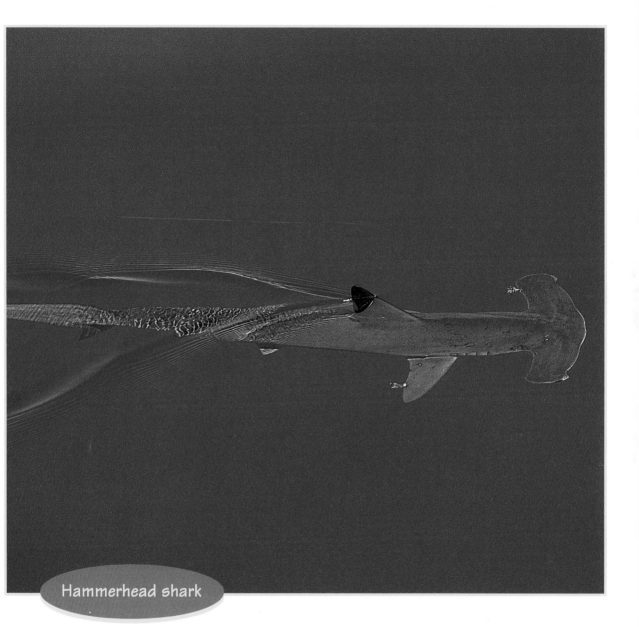

Hammerhead shark

What Sixth Sense Do Hammerheads Have?

Sharks have the same five senses that you have. They can see, hear, smell, taste, and feel. But hammerheads—and all other sharks—have a sixth sense. It is called electroreception (ih LEHK troh rih SEHP shuhn).

Few fish have this special sense. Pores on the skin of a shark's head lead to sensory tubes. The tubes can detect the small amounts of electricity coming from the bodies of smaller fish and other creatures. The shark can pinpoint the exact location of prey and quickly close in for the kill.

Electroreception can also act like a compass. This helps sharks make their way through the water. It also helps them migrate, or move long distances.

In addition to their special electroreception, sharks have very good vision. They can even see in the dim light of deep waters. Their hearing is excellent, too. It helps them locate prey.

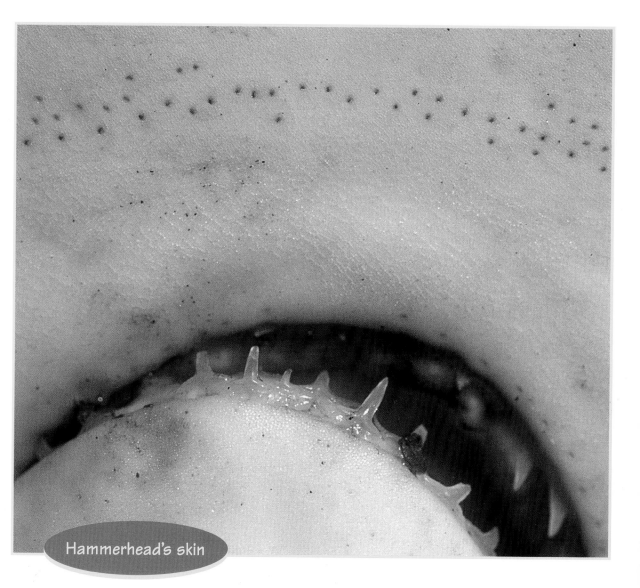

Hammerhead's skin

Do Hammerheads Like to Be Together?

They seem to. One of the most awesome sights in the ocean is a school of hammerheads swimming together.

For some reason, hammerheads come together only at certain times of the year. And they gather only in certain places, such as the Gulf of California in Mexico and the Galapagos (*guh LAH puh GOHS*) Islands in South America.

For years, people off Myrtle Beach, South Carolina, watched schools of hammerheads as they migrated south. Hurricane Hugo disturbed those waters in 1989, causing the hammerheads to change their migration path.

No one knows for sure why hammerheads come together in groups. Shark experts think that they may do so to migrate, to mate, or to hunt together in shallow waters.

Large school of
hammerheads

Are Hammerheads a Danger to People?

They can be. Hammerheads eat fish and shellfish. They do not attack people for food, but they will defend themselves from people when they need to.

Attacks on humans by hammerheads and other sharks are actually very rare. Only about 50 kinds of sharks are dangerous to people. Worldwide, fewer than 50 shark attacks were reported each year between 1990 and 1996. Only about 6 of those attacks resulted in the victim's death.

Still, people do need to be careful when swimming in waters where sharks are numerous. The most important thing to remember is to stay calm. Don't start splashing and kicking. Swim away with slow, strong strokes.

Hammerhead shark
with scuba diver

21

Is the Great White the Most Dangerous Shark?

Yes! The great white shark has probably been responsible for more attacks on people than any other shark, including the hammerhead. Attacks have occurred most frequently along the coasts of California, southern Australia, New Zealand, and South Africa.

Oddly enough, most of these attacks were probably mistakes on the shark's part. The great white's favorite prey include sea lions and seals. When swimming, a person looks very much like a seal, and this may explain the attacks.

Even when bitten by a great white, a swimmer often has a good chance of survival. The great white usually takes a bite of its victim and then retreats. Some scientists believe the shark may be waiting for its victim to bleed to death. Others think the shark may find that a human is an unsuitable meal. In any case, during this time, the injured swimmer can often be rescued or swim to safety.

Great white shark

What Makes the Great White So Great?

The great white shark has great size. It can grow to a length of 21 feet (6.4 meters). Also, it has great teeth. But, most of all, the great white shark has great speed and tremendous strength.

Most fish have temperatures that are the same as the water in which they are swimming. But a few sharks, including the great white, can keep their bodies warmer than the water. Warm blood flows in and around the muscles. This helps the shark swim faster. It also helps with those sudden bursts of speed that are useful in chasing prey.

While the great white is indeed great, it is not completely white. Young great white sharks have brown coloring on their backs. Old ones are partly gray or blue.

Great white shark attacking

25

Are All Sharks Dangerous?

No. In fact, the largest shark of all is known as the "gentle giant" of the deep. It is the whale shark. A whale shark may reach a length of 40 feet (12 meters). That's about as long as a bus. The whale shark may weigh about 13 short tons (11.8 metric tons). That's the size of two African elephants put together! Whale sharks lay eggs that are the size of footballs!

A whale shark is dark gray or reddish in color. It has a broad, flat head and a wide mouth. It has over 300 rows of tiny, hooked teeth.

You might think such a giant of a shark would be a threat to humans. A whale shark, however, is harmless—except to the plankton that are its prey.

Whale shark
with scuba diver

Why Do Whale Sharks Stand Up to Eat?

Whale sharks eat tiny plankton and fish that live near the surface of the water. To catch their prey, whale sharks swim near the surface with their mouths wide open. Whale sharks can also "stand" vertically in the water, with heads up and mouths open. These sharks take great amounts of water in through their mouths. They filter out the plankton and tiny fish through large, spongelike gills.

Unfortunately, the habit of standing has caused some whale sharks to be injured or killed by boats that accidentally ram into them.

Whale shark "standing" in water

Do Basking Sharks Really Bask?

Not really—they just look as if they do. Like whale sharks, basking sharks swim near the ocean's surface in order to eat tiny plankton. They may look as if they are basking, or warming themselves, in the sun. But basking sharks are actually swimming slowly and filtering water through their gills. An adult basking shark can filter out about 2,400 gallons (9,000 liters) of water in an hour!

A basking shark may measure over 30 feet (9.1 meters) in length. This makes it the second largest shark. Like a whale shark, it poses no danger to humans.

Basking shark

Why Do Nurse Sharks Like the Ocean Floor?

Nurse sharks find their favorite foods—crab, lobster, and shrimp—on the ocean floor. While whale and basking sharks feed near the surface of the ocean, nurse sharks feed on the ocean bottom. They lie there without moving, waiting for prey to come near.

Unlike many other sharks, a nurse shark does not need constant motion to breathe. It breathes in a different way. Opening and closing its mouth makes a muscle expand and contract. The muscle acts like a valve in the nurse shark's throat. This "pump action" keeps water and oxygen flowing, even when the nurse shark isn't moving.

The habit of staying motionless in shallow water makes nurse sharks a danger to people. Thinking they were a different kind of fish, swimmers have tried to capture nurse sharks by their tails. These swimmers have been attacked.

Nurse shark

Which Is the Smallest Shark?

Lantern sharks include some of the smallest sharks. In fact, the dwarf lantern shark is the smallest known shark. It grows only 8 inches (20 centimeters) long and weighs only 1/2 ounce (15 grams).

Lantern sharks are deep-water feeders that eat shellfish and small squid. These sharks are members of the dogfish family of sharks. Most of them are small and slender.

The belly of a lantern shark lights up like a lantern. That is how this shark got its name. Many small light organs are embedded in the skin of the lantern shark's belly. The light lantern sharks give off may help attract prey.

Lantern shark

How Do Saw Sharks Use Their Saws?

The sawlike snout on this saw shark looks like a dangerous weapon, doesn't it? Actually it's not. The saw shark uses its long, pointed snout more like a rake than a weapon.

A saw shark uses its barbels *(BAHR buhlz)* to detect the small bony fish it likes to eat. Barbels are those long, fleshy barbs that grow from the sides of the shark's mouth. When its barbels sense prey, the saw shark uses its snout to stir up the sand. This brings the prey out of hiding, and the saw shark quickly captures its dinner.

Most saw sharks live off the coast of southern Australia. They are usually shy and harmless. They will, however, strike out at anyone who tries to handle their snouts. Since saw sharks grow to about 5 feet (1.5 meters) in length, it's best to leave them alone—even if they seem harmless.

Saw shark

Are Goblin Sharks Really Scary?

Think about this description and you decide. A goblin shark has a long snout, similar to that of the saw shark. The shovel-shaped snout hangs over its jaws. Long, needlelike teeth stick out from an expandable mouth that is one of the largest of any shark. Is that scary enough for you?

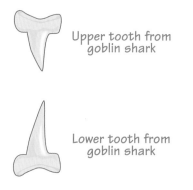

Upper tooth from goblin shark

Lower tooth from goblin shark

Goblin sharks were thought to be extinct. Then in the 1890's, one was caught off the coast of Japan. Since then this strange shark has also been found in deep waters off South America, Europe, southern Australia, and Asia.

Goblin shark

39

How Do Thresher Sharks Use Their Tails?

Many sharks, such as hammerheads and saw sharks, use their heads to capture prey. Thresher sharks, however, use their tails.

Thresher sharks grow to 20 feet (6.1 meters) in length. Nearly half of this length is tail. When a thresher finds a school of small fish, it whips its tail around the fish. It swims in smaller and smaller circles—enclosing the fish. The fish panic and draw themselves into an even tighter circle. When the fish are packed very tightly together, the thresher shark moves in for the kill. It quickly snatches a meal with its sharp teeth.

Thresher shark

How Did the Cookie Cutter Shark Get Its Name?

Its name may sound cute, but it comes from the grisly method this shark uses to attack its prey. These sharks are only about 20 inches (50 centimeters) long. But unlike most sharks, cookie cutter sharks prey on fish that are larger than themselves. They also attack dolphins, seals, and even whales.

A cookie cutter shark latches onto its prey with its sucking mouth. Then it sinks its sharp lower teeth into the fish and twists around. It carves out a plug of flesh, using its teeth like a cookie cutter.

Sometimes sharks attack prey so forcefully that they break and swallow their own teeth. A cookie cutter shark does this. It is common to find one with a whole row of teeth in its stomach.

42

Cookie cutter shark

Is There Anything Tiger Sharks Will Not Eat?

Tiger sharks will try almost any food. A tiger shark's diet includes fish of all kinds, other sharks, crabs, sea snakes, turtles, and sea lions. The tiger shark will eat dead, floating animals and snatch sea gulls off the water's surface. It will even eat cardboard boxes and other garbage floating in the water near coastal cities!

Although it is as ferocious as the animal it is named for, the tiger shark has no stripes! It has spotted markings.

Tiger shark

How Do Zebra Sharks Protect Their Eggs?

Zebra sharks are another type of shark named after a land animal. A young zebra shark has stripes like a zebra. But the stripes gradually break up into spots as the shark grows older.

Like many other sharks, a zebra shark lays its eggs in tough, leathery egg cases. It uses long, barblike threads to attach the egg cases to coral, rocks, and other objects on the ocean floor. This helps to protect the eggs and keep them safe from predators.

In time, the baby zebra sharks hatch. They split open the cases, which often wash up on shore where people find them. The egg cases are called mermaids' purses.

Zebra shark

Why Do Fishing Crews Hate Blue Sharks?

While most sharks hunt their own food, blue sharks often let fishing crews do the hunting for them.

The powerful blue shark follows schools of herring, tuna, and sardines. Fishing crews use large nets to catch these school of fish. All too often, a blue shark will rip open the nets. The shark will then help itself to the catch.

Blue sharks sometimes become trapped in the fishing nets. The fishing crews will then capture the sharks and send them to be processed for food.

Blue shark

Which Shark Is the Speed Demon of the Deep?

It's the mako. This shark's streamlined body is perfect for speed. Mako sharks can swim really fast—about 22 miles (35 kilometers) per hour. In short bursts, they may even be able to reach speeds of 35 miles (56 kilometers) per hour.

In addition to being speedy, makos are quite acrobatic. They are one of only a few types of sharks that leap out of the water—sometimes quite high. Makos can stop, turn, and speed up quite suddenly. About the only thing they cannot do is swim backward. But no sharks can do that.

Because of their speed and agility, makos are a favorite of people who fish for sport. When caught, a mako may struggle for hours, jumping and fighting to get free. The people fishing seem to enjoy the challenge of capturing this great predator after a long struggle.

Mako shark

What Are Bull Sharks Doing in Lakes and Rivers?

They are looking for food, of course. Unlike most sharks that can live only in salt water, bull sharks can adapt to the fresh water of rivers and lakes.

Bull sharks have been found hundreds of miles from the sea in major rivers such as the Amazon in Brazil, the Ganges *(GAN jeez)* in India, and even the Mississippi River in the United States. Bull sharks have also been discovered in lakes with access to the sea, such as Lake Jamoer in Indonesia *(in deh NEE zhuh)* and Lake Nicaragua *(NIHK uh RAH gwuh)* in Central America.

While hunting fish and other sharks, bull sharks have been known to attack swimmers.

Bull shark

Which Is the "Newest" Shark in the Sea?

Maybe *newest* is not the right word. Much of the world's vast ocean is still unexplored. Sharks that have been living there for millions of years are regularly being discovered.

One of the latest discoveries is the megamouth shark. A megamouth was first seen in 1976. Since then, several others have been found. In 1990, one survived being caught in a fishing net near Los Angeles, California. The 16-foot (4.9-meter) shark would have died if kept in captivity. So a team of scientists implanted transmitters in its head and released it. The scientists then tracked the shark's movement at sea for several days.

The megamouth, as its name suggests, has a huge mouth and gigantic jaws. But it uses them to eat only tiny plankton. As other megamouths are found and studied, scientists will learn more about this "newest" shark.

Megamouth shark

Who's That Hiding in the Seaweed?

It's a shark—disguised as seaweed! Many animals have colors and patterns that help them blend into their surroundings. Most animals use this camouflage to hide from predators. But sharks are different. They camouflage themselves from prey.

Take this tasseled wobbegong *(WOH buh gong),* for example. It has many branched lobes, or tassels, around its mouth. When the wobbegong lies in seaweed, its tassels wave just like the seaweed. Unsuspecting shrimp and fish swim by—only to be gobbled up by the wobbegong.

Another shark that hides from prey is the angel shark. It covers its flat body with sand and hides on the sandy ocean floor.

Not all sharks use camouflage to hide from prey. Some small sharks hide from predators. The swell shark's brown blotches help it hide among rocks. If danger is nearby, it will even wedge itself into a crevice by puffing out its stomach.

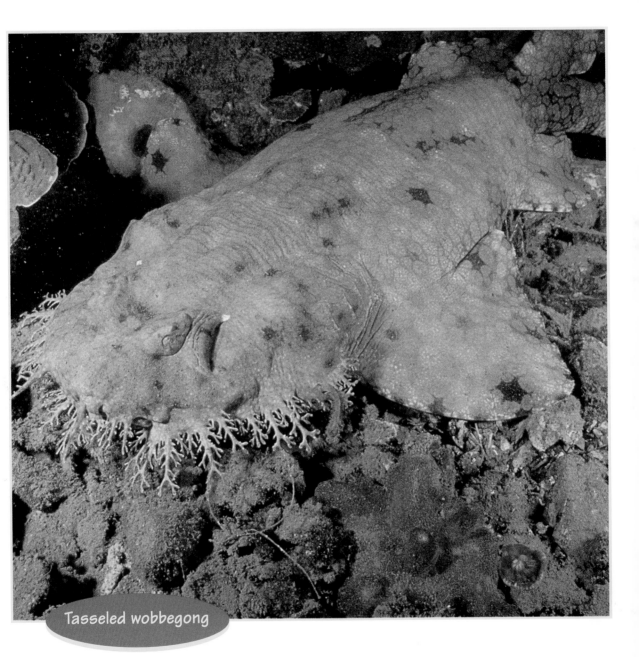

Tasseled wobbegong

What Can We Learn from Sharks?

Surprisingly, we might learn how to live longer. Many scientists believe sharks are among the healthiest creatures in the sea. Sharks rarely get cancer or other diseases. For many years, scientists have been studying sharks to learn about the excellent immune system in their bodies. The scientists hope that they will be able to use this knowledge to make humans just as resistant to disease.

We can also learn about how the ocean's environment works from studying sharks. Sharks are the highest link in the ocean's food chain. They help to keep the population of different fishes at normal levels. They also help keep the ocean clean by eating dead and diseased fish.

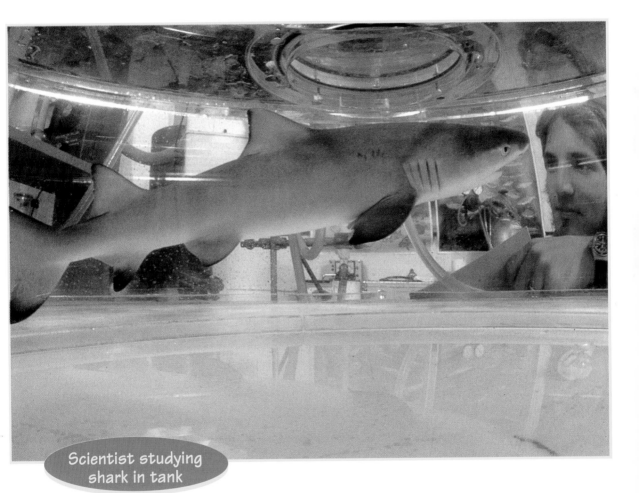

Scientist studying
shark in tank

Are Sharks in Danger?

People may fear sharks, but sharks have much more reason to fear people. Over 30 million sharks are killed by people each year.

Some sharks are killed for their meat, liver oil, or skins. Others are killed simply for sport. Among the most threatened sharks today are makos, basking sharks, and great white sharks.

Most sharks have very low birth rates. This means that each year sharks have very few young. When too many adults of one kind are killed, survivors may not be able to raise enough young to keep the species from becoming extinct.

Some countries have passed laws to protect endangered sharks. Perhaps the best way to save sharks is to educate people about them. We should realize that sharks are not "bad" animals. Although they eat other fish to survive, sharks are an important part of their environment, and they pose little danger to humans.

Great white shark

Shark Fun Facts

→ A hammerhead's favorite food is a dangerous dish—the stingray. One hammerhead was found to have 50 stingray stingers in its jaw.

→ Shark teeth are replaceable. There are rows of teeth behind the front set that move into place when needed.

→ Nurse sharks and a few others begin to prey even before they are born. One of the first to hatch inside the mother will eat the other young and eggs.

→ Spiny dogfish live longer than any other sharks. These sharks have been known to live 70 years.

→ Newborn sharks are called pups. Unlike dogs, sharks give little or no care to their young. Some sharks eat their own pups!

→ The great white shark is related to an even more ferocious shark that lived over 60 million years ago. Jaws of this huge shark have been found with teeth 6 inches (15 centimeters) long!

Glossary

carnivore A meat-eating animal.

cartilage A strong, lightweight, stretchy material not as hard as bone.

compass An instrument for showing directions.

egg case The covering around an egg.

electroreception A shark's sense that feels electricity from prey.

endangered In danger of dying out.

extinct Died out and never seen again.

fins Winglike parts of a fish's body that help it swim and balance in water.

gills Openings in a fish's head for breathing in water.

immune system Body parts that protect from disease.

mammal An animal that is warm-blooded and has a backbone. Female mammals produce milk to feed their young.

nutrient Food for growing.

oxygen A gas in the air that people and animals need to breathe.

plankton Very small plants and animals that float in seas and lakes.

pores Very small openings.

prey Animals that other animals eat.

primitive Very simple, not developed.

school A large group of the same kind of water animals swimming together.

shark A torpedo-shaped fish that mostly lives in the sea.

species A group of the same kind of animals.

swim bladder An internal body sac that fills with air and helps keep fish afloat in water.

yolk Food in an egg.

Index

Picture Acknowledgments: Front & Back Cover: © Ron & Valerie Taylor, Bruce Coleman Inc.; © Michel Jozon, Innerspace Visions; © Amos Nachoum, Innerspace Visions; © Doug Perrine, Innerspace Visions; © David Shen, Innerspace Visions.

© Abrahms Bahm, Bruce Coleman Inc. 53; © Ferrari/Watt from Innerspace Visions 41; © David Fleetham, Innerspace Visions 23; © François Gohier, Photo Researchers 15; © Howard Hall, Innerspace Visions 31, 51; © Richard Hermann, Innerspace Visions 49; © Michel Jozon, Innerspace Visions 57; © Rudie Kuiter 13; © Gwen Lowe, Innerspace Visions 43; © Amos Nachoum, Innerspace Visions 25, 61; © Flip Nicklin, Minden Pictures 59; © Gregory Ochocki, Photo Researchers 33; © Doug Perrine, Innerspace Visions 17, 21, 45, 47; © Bruce Rasner, Innerspace Visions 55; © Ed Robinson, Tom Stack & Associates 27; © Jeff Rotman, Innerspace Visions 11, 35; © David Shen, Innerspace Visions 39; Marty Snyderman, 4, 19, 37; © Ron & Valerie Taylor, Bruce Coleman Inc. 3, 7.

Illustrations: WORLD BOOK illustration by Michael DiGiorgio 9, 38; WORLD BOOK illustration by Patricia Stein 62.